MW01136840

WOMEN IN SCIENCE

GRACE HOPPER

COMPUTER SCIENTIST

By Jill C. Wheeler

Content Consultant
Dr. C. Dianne Martin
Professor Emeritus of Computer Science
George Washington University

Essential Library

An Imprint of Abdo Publishing | abdopublishing.com

ABDOPUBLISHING.COM

Published by Abdo Publishing, a division of ABDO, PO Box 398166, Minneapolis, Minnesota 55439. Copyright © 2018 by Abdo Consulting Group, Inc. International copyrights reserved in all countries. No part of this book may be reproduced in any form without written permission from the publisher. Essential Library™ is a trademark and logo of Abdo Publishing.

Printed in the United States of America, North Mankato, Minnesota
042017
092017

Cover Photo: AP Images
Interior Photos: Bettmann/Getty Images, 4, 77, 91; Claudio Divizia/iStockphoto, 9; ClassicStock.com/SuperStock, 14, 68; Grace Murray Hopper Collection/Archives Center/ National Museum of American History/Smithsonian Institution, 16, 34, 44, 53, 54, 57, 63; George Grantham Bain Collection/Library of Congress, 23; Vassarion 1928/Archives and Special Collections/Vassar College, 24; Ferd, Mayor & Co./Library of Congress, 26; PH2 David C. MacLean/US Navy, 28; iStockphoto, 32–33, 60; Cynthia Johnson/The LIFE Images Collection/Getty Images, 37, 85; Alfred T. Palmer/Office of War Information/ Overseas Picture Division/Library of Congress, 42–43; PhotoQuest/Archive Photos/ Getty Images, 50; Naval History and Heritage Command, 59; Michael Poche/AP Images, 64; Boyer/Roger Viollet/Getty Images, 65; Science Source, 66; Gift of Grace Hopper, Division of Medicine & Science, National Museum of American History, Smithsonian Institution, 75; John Preito/Denver Post/Getty Images, 78; US Navy Naval Aviation News, 81; Lee Jin-man/AP Images, 87; Department of Defense/AP Images, 88; Peter Southwick/ AP Images, 92; Mass Communication Specialist 2nd Class Jon Dasbach/US Navy, 94–95

Editor: Susan E. Hamen
Series Designer: Nikki Farinella

PUBLISHER'S CATALOGING–IN–PUBLICATION DATA

Names: Wheeler, Jill C., author.
Title: Grace Hopper: computer scientist / by Jill C. Wheeler.
Other titles: Computer scientist
Description: Minneapolis, MN : Abdo Publishing, 2018. | Series: Women in
    science | Includes bibliographical references and index.
Identifiers: LCCN 2016962270 | ISBN 9781532110443 (lib. bdg.) |
    ISBN 9781680788297 (ebook)
Subjects: LCSH: Hopper, Grace Murray--Juvenile literature. | Women computer
    engineers--United States--Biography--Juvenile literature. | Admirals--United
    States--Biography--Juvenile literature. | United States.--Navy--Biography--
    Juvenile literature.
Classification: DDC 004/.092 [B]--dc23
LC record available at http://lccn.loc.gov/2016962270

CONTENTS

THERE'S GOT TO BE A BETTER WAY

The summer of 1949 found Grace Hopper frustrated. She had a PhD in mathematics from Yale University. Yet she could not get her checkbook to balance. After several months of struggling, she asked her brother, Roger, for help. Roger pored over the columns of her checkbook register, checking and rechecking. Roger realized that sometimes Hopper subtracted correctly, but other times she did not. Finally, he realized the problem. His sister had been mixing up normal numbers with octal, a mathematical system based on eight digits instead of the standard base of ten.

Roger's findings got Hopper thinking. Since June 1949, she had been working for the Eckert-Mauchly Computer Corporation, or EMCC, as a senior mathematician. The start-up

Grace Hopper, a leader in the computer programming field, helped change the way computers receive data and provide feedback.

computer company had asked Hopper to write coding instructions to run programs on its Binary Automatic Computer (BINAC), which was being developed for Northrop Aircraft Corporation's secret Snark Missile project. BINAC was able to perform high-speed arithmetic and was the world's first computer that contained stored programs. It contained approximately 700 vacuum tubes and was too large to easily move once it was set up. Each workday, the 42-year-old Hopper lived in a world of octal, converting base-ten numbers into

The First Computer

English mathematician Charles Babbage is credited with being among the first people to talk about building a calculating machine. In the early 1820s, Babbage was frustrated with the unreliability of printed tables used for calculations. Such tables commonly were used for everything from navigation to banking to construction. Yet the tables were not perfect. They contained errors caused by miscopying or miscalculations.

Babbage dreamed of a way to automate creation of these tables, which would remove such errors. He believed machines, unlike humans, would not make mistakes in their calculations. In 1822, he drew up designs for a "difference engine" that would add numbers. However, because he lacked funding and a skilled machinist who could craft it to his specifications, he was not able to build it.

Babbage had assistance in his work from young mentee Ada Lovelace. In writing about Babbage's designs, Lovelace described how codes could be created so the machine could handle letters and symbols as well as numbers. She also came up with the theory of looping, which is when a computer repeats a series of instructions. For these and other contributions, Lovelace is often referred to as the first computer programmer.

their base-eight equivalents so she could enter them into the computer. At that time, octal was considered to be the most efficient way to accomplish the task. Yet outside of the office, Hopper needed to use the conventional base-ten system.

Hopper realized she had two choices. Either she could become better at the language the computer was using, or the computer could become better at the language *she* was using. She decided it would be more efficient to teach the computer how to process language that was more familiar to people. Hopper would soon shift focus to work on another computer using a different programming language. But the core desire to make computers communicate with people more easily stuck with her.

PROGRAMMING THE UNIVAC

In mid-1949, Hopper moved from working on the BINAC to a different project at EMCC called UNIVAC, for Universal Automatic Computer. In the eyes of EMCC founders and former professors John Mauchly and J. Presper Eckert, UNIVAC was going to revolutionize computers. They envisioned a high-speed electronic digital computer with an ability to work with problems that involved both numbers and words. Early computers could only work with numbers, which limited their abilities. If they could be redesigned to compute words as well, computers would become an exciting new tool for businesses

Octal vs. Decimal

Octal is a number system consisting of eight single-digit numbers: zero, one, two, three, four, five, six, and seven. It is a base-eight system, in contrast to the base-ten system that people use commonly. When she worked with BINAC, Hopper had to convert decimal numbers into octal equivalents. BINAC would then convert the octal numbers into binary code, which consists of two numbers, zero and one. The zeros and ones worked like on and off switches, with one being on and zero being off. Binary code could run faster than coding of normal numbers.

Even today's computers store information and operate in binary. Yet in 1949, data was still being entered largely by people tapping numbers on keypads. Entering information in binary takes a lot of time and numbers. Octal helped reduce the size of those numbers. For example, the number ten in binary must be entered as "1010." In octal, it must be entered as "12." That change saved time and reduced the potential for mistakes.

to use as well as for scientific purposes. "He [Mauchly] was envisioning much larger problems which hadn't even been stated yet," Hopper recalled. "He was visualizing the use of computers in the business and industrial area, the things that they would be able to do."[1]

Hopper had become head of the software division at EMCC, and she was assigned to program UNIVAC. A programmer provided the computer with a list of instructions to carry out. This was done using a punch card, which was a stiff piece of paper with holes punched in specific patterns that represented data. These were inserted into the computer, which read the holes in the cards and translated them into information. Hopper hired a team of four men and four women to assist her in building a collection of

SCIENCE
SPOTLIGHT

PUNCH CARDS

Modern computers allow users to save files, which can be opened and changed at any time. However, when Hopper was beginning to work with computers, data was accessed by inserting a punch card into the computer. Punch cards were created by inserting a thick paper card into a punch card machine. Holes were then punched in columns to represent characters. Once the punch card was completed, the desired data was stored on the card. One drawback of the punch card was that it held a limited number of holes, and therefore limited data. If a large amount of data needed to be stored, multiple cards were necessary. It was crucial that the cards remained in a stack in the correct order so that the machine could read the data in the correct order. When the user loaded the program, each card was inserted into a punch card reader that input the data from the cards into the computer.

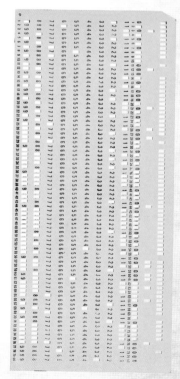

Punch cards date back to the early 1700s. Textile looms could be controlled by punch cards. The loom followed a sequence of operations based on white punch cards with holes and wove patterns based on the data the cards provided. In 1725, a French weaver named Joseph-Marie Jacquard used punch cards to create a self-portrait woven in silk.

useful punch cards containing information for UNIVAC. Some of the team members were people she had worked with before. EMCC was building the first UNIVAC computer, which was to be used by the US Census Bureau.

Hopper and her team made the UNIVAC project a success. The computer was able to work with both numerical and alphabetical data inputs. It was also the first computer to separate input and output. The new computer featured a code that was closer to Hopper's vision of how humans and computers could communicate. "John Mauchly wrote the C-10 code [assembly language] for the UNIVAC I, and it has been the basis of most codes since," Hopper recalled years later. "'A' was add, 'M' was multiply, 'B' was bring, 'C' was clear; it was a beautiful code."[2] The first UNIVAC computer was delivered to the US Census Bureau in 1951.

TEACHING COMPUTERS TO UNDERSTAND HUMANS

Hopper continued to think about how to make it faster and easier for humans to work with computers. In May 1952, Hopper presented a paper at a meeting of the Association for Computing Machinery in Pittsburgh, Pennsylvania. The paper outlined a new and radical idea. Why not teach machines how to assemble their programs, instead of having humans input every step of each program? Hopper's paper suggested that computers could be given sets of instructions on how to perform simple, common tasks. She called these simple tasks *subroutines*. In many ways, programmers were already working in this way. Programmers often used the same short sets of instructions to create more complex programs. Yet each time they created a new program, they had to input the subroutines yet again, which took a lot of time and often resulted in mistakes.

Hopper proposed that these subroutines could be thought about like books in a library. Each subroutine told the computer how to do something. By organizing the subroutines into a catalog, users could tell the computer which subroutines it needed to look up and in what order to do its job. Hopper finished her description of this new program generator by

The US Census Bureau: Computer-Innovation Pioneer

EMCC's first UNIVAC computer was funded by the US Census Bureau. Beginning in 1790, the bureau was charged with tracking population demographics to determine how congressional seats should be allocated. Yet by 1880, there were more people in the United States than could be effectively counted by the bureau's manual data-processing abilities. As it was, 1,500 clerks worked more than seven years to produce the bureau's report. The bureau turned to engineer Herman Hollerith for assistance in tabulating results of the 1890 census. Hollerith developed a system to record a person's identifying information as a series of holes punched in cards, which could then be read by machines. Hollerith went on to become one of the founders of the company later known as International Business Machines (IBM). The Census Bureau used UNIVAC to tabulate part of the 1950 population census, along with the entire 1954 economic census.

calling it a compiler. That was because it compiled subroutines into a program the same way librarians compile books from a collection into a bibliography. Hopper was so excited about her ideas that she made 200 copies of her presentation and left them at the back of the room for people to take. However, half of them were still there when it was time to leave.

ADDRESSING THE SKEPTICS

Hopper refused to let the lukewarm response stop her from promoting her idea. She continued to talk about the benefits of her new system. She talked about writing and testing computer programs in hours instead of weeks. She noted how the programs would be more accurate, too. That was because programmers already would have cleaned up any mistakes in the subroutines. Some people were excited by Hopper's ideas. Others remained skeptical. The skeptics told Hopper that computers could only do arithmetic. They could never write their own programs.

Even Hopper's employer, Remington Rand, which had purchased EMCC in 1950, had little interest in Hopper's ideas. Hopper and her colleagues had to work on the project in their spare time. By the summer of 1952, they had their first functioning compiler, which they named A-0. The A stood for Algebraic. They began testing the compiler by pitting it against the work of human programmers. One experiment took the UNIVAC with the A-0 compiler less than 49 minutes. It took the human programming team 880 minutes to do the same task.

Compiler versions A-1 and A-2 soon followed. Each was a little better than the one before. Hopper and her team found themselves talking to buyers of UNIVACs about the benefits of these compilers. Computer compilers take the programming language that is produced by people and convert it into the binary language that the machine is able to understand. Computers within the same model family would have the same low-level language and could use the same compiler. This meant that with the use of a compiler, a program could work on different machines of the same model. That meant less

Meet the UNIVAC

UNIVAC was the first mass-produced commercial computer, introduced in 1951. A total of 46 UNIVAC I (the first generation) computers were built. In today's dollars, the machine would have cost $7 million. The room-sized UNIVAC was 25 feet (7.6 m) tall and 50 feet (15 m) long and weighed approximately 17,000 pounds (7,711 kg). It used 5,600 vacuum tubes, 18,000 crystal diodes, and 300 relays.[3] It was the first computer to have digital magnetic tape, though it also could use punch cards. Digital magnetic tape was a long, narrow strip of plastic film that was coated with a magnetic material. Information could be stored on the magnetic tape. Users could erase data and reuse the tape to record new data.

A UNIVAC machine accurately predicted the winner of the 1952 presidential election before the polls closed. It did so by running a program that compared the 1952 returns to previous election returns and outcomes to predict which way the election was trending.

Early computers like the UNIVAC were much larger than modern computers, often filling up an entire room.

time was needed for programming, and there was less demand for programmers, already in short supply. As more and more computers entered the world of business, that was an important feature. However, as with any new technology, many people were slow to adopt the compiler program. Some programmers were afraid the compilers would take away their jobs. Others simply never got around to trying the new technology.

Hopper liked to tell the story of a programmer who had to run a mathematical project for a big corporate meeting the following day. The programmer was running out of time and was desperate. He used the A-2 compiler for the first time, even though he could have tried it for months. The man was able to complete the project on time, which led to a promotion and a raise. "Everybody started to use the compiler," Hopper recalled. "It's a wonderful thing what a raise will do."[4] Hopper received a number of letters from people who told her how much time and effort the compiler saved them. The letters were the beginning of a legacy that would span more than four decades and touch countless lives.

Mathematics in Everyday Life

Mathematics deals with the logic of shape, quantity, and arrangement, so it is foundational to our lives— from the buildings we live and study in to the mobile phones we use and how we handle our money. So many of the technologies people take for granted every day would be impossible without mathematics.

Cell phones, navigation systems, personal computers, and Wi-Fi all rely on mathematics, specifically algorithms, to function. In these examples, an algorithm is a step-by-step process for solving a problem. Algorithms encrypt and compress voice data as it leaves cell phones. They help navigation systems figure out the shortest distance between two points. They help keep Wi-Fi routers secure. Facebook feeds and Netflix movie recommendations would be impossible without algorithms and the mathematics behind them. Not all algorithms are created equal, however. Hopper and other programmers learned early on that the best algorithms were those that were simple, already tested, and took up the least amount of the computer's memory, which was especially limited in the early days of the field.

WELCOME, GRACE

G race Hopper was born Grace Brewster Murray on December 9, 1906, in New York City, New York. Her mother, Mary Campbell Van Horne Murray, named her oldest daughter after her best friend, Grace Brewster. Hopper was the first child born to Mary and her husband, Walter Fletcher Murray, an insurance broker. Three years later, a sister, Mary, joined the family. Grace's brother, Roger, was born in 1911. The Murray children were born into a wealthy family. Similar to other families in their social class, they had nannies and maids. Grace was born in her grandparents' home, yet she was just a few weeks old when her parents moved into their own apartment at 316 West 95th Street. It was a home that would

Grace Hopper's parents encouraged their children to receive a good education and pursue their dreams.

be filled with books, questions, and intellectual exploration as Grace and her siblings grew.

By the time of Grace's birth, both the Murray and Van Horne families were well established in the United States. Grace's paternal grandfather had arrived from Scotland at age 11. He had carved out a successful career in the insurance industry. Grace's mother's family had been in America since before the Revolutionary War. Her mother's father, John Van Horne, was the chief civil engineer for the city of New York in the late 1800s. John sometimes took his daughter, Grace's mother, to work with him as he computed angles and laid out the city's streets. In later years, he took young Grace with him. She recalls enjoying these expeditions when she was allowed to lend a hand by holding up the red-and-white striped surveyor's pole. Grace thought about

An Alarming Curiosity

Grace frequently shared a story from her childhood that highlighted her early interest in technology. Her family's summer cottage in New Hampshire had seven bedrooms, and each bedroom had an alarm clock complete with a large bell on top. Grace recalls being fascinated by the clock in her bedroom, so she decided to take it apart to see how it worked. Unfortunately, when she unscrewed the back cover, the inner workings tumbled onto the floor. Grace then began taking the clocks from the other rooms and opening them up to see how they worked. She took all seven clocks apart, but recalled that she was unable to determine exactly how the clocks worked. Her mother eventually restricted her daughter to playing with one clock.

Women and Education in the Early 1900s

When Grace was going through school, it was customary for young women from wealthy families to complete their education, work for several years, then quit their jobs to marry and start a family. Some employers even had rules against employing married women. This was in part because many people questioned whether women could balance a career with family life.

Grace's own mother faced this discrimination in her early years. Mary Murray showed a talent for mathematics and studied it as much as was allowed. However, in the late 1800s it was considered improper for women to study advanced mathematics. Mary married and was never able to pursue a mathematics career.

becoming an engineer before starting college, yet she gave up the idea, noting that "there was no place for women in engineering at that time."[1]

EQUAL EDUCATION OPPORTUNITIES

Such societal attitudes were not held inside the Murray household. Both of Grace's parents believed their daughters should have the same educational opportunities as their son. Their commitment to education grew even more in 1915. Walter Murray suffered from a condition known as hardening of the arteries. The condition is caused when blood vessels carrying oxygen-rich blood from the heart become narrowed. In Walter, the condition reduced the oxygen and blood supply to his legs. The only treatment option at that time was to cut off his legs. Even with the amputations, he and Mary were not sure how long he would live with so many circulation problems. They felt it was important that their children be able to support themselves. As it turned out, Walter lived for many more years, dying at age 74. He continued his successful insurance business even as he got around on wooden legs with his socks thumb-tacked to the wood to hold them up. Mary, meanwhile, quickly learned how to drive so she could take her husband to work and back. She also took on household jobs that had once belonged to her husband.

As the oldest child, Grace was expected to be the most responsible one. That was not always the case. She recalls a summer adventure climbing trees with her cousins. It was an outing that got them in trouble with the adults. "Since I was at the top, it was obvious who started it," she said.[2] At the same time, she loved learning and reading as well

New York to New Hampshire

From the age of six months until World War II (1939–1945), Grace spent each summer at the family's summer cottage on Lake Wentworth in Wolfeboro, New Hampshire. Her family was one of multiple Murray families that owned property on that lakeshore, eventually leading to its nickname as the New York shore. The area remained relatively quiet for many years because of its remoteness. To get there, the Hopper family had to take the night boat from New York to Fall River, Massachusetts. The next day they took a train to South Station in Boston, Massachusetts, then a trolley across Boston to the North Station. From there, they took a train to Sanbornville, New Hampshire, and another train along the shore of Lake Wentworth. In later years, the family was able to drive, but the trip took even longer because the roads were unpaved.

as the outdoors. She and her extended family spent many long summers at their cottage on Lake Wentworth in New Hampshire. There, Grace and her siblings, cousins, and friends sailed on the lake, played games, swam, and hiked.

Grace and her siblings also learned what their mother considered important life skills. Each child kept a vegetable garden and learned how to sew and cook. Grace also became quite skilled at needlework and knitting, which she continued throughout her life. In later years, professional colleagues would recount that Grace would be busily knitting or embroidering even in the middle of meetings. They soon learned that her industriousness did not mean she was not listening to the conversation. She would pipe up to answer questions without stopping the clicking of her needles.

Back in New York City, Mary Murray took her children to visit all of the city's

Remember the Admiral

Grace liked to speak of her great-grandfather John H. Russell, who had served in the Union navy during the US Civil War (1861–1865). He retired from the navy in 1886 after having reached the rank of rear admiral. Grace met him once as a child, but the memory remained. Her mother also liked to remind her of Russell's accomplishments. Grace told the story of a day at the family's summer home when her mother was watching Grace maneuver the family's sail canoe on Lake Wentworth. Suddenly a gust of wind capsized the boat, sending Grace into the water. Her mother calmly reached for the megaphone she kept nearby and called to her daughter, "Remember your great-grandfather the admiral."[3] Grace was able to cling to the upturned canoe and kick it—and herself—safely back to shore.

best museums, lectures, and concerts. She and her husband also saw to it that their children participated in the family's lively dinnertime discussions. Even the youngest family members were encouraged to share their ideas and opinions. Grace said she learned how to make arguments and back them up during family dinners. It was a skill that would serve her well in her career.

PRIVATE SCHOOLS

Similar to many other children from upper-middle-class families, Grace attended private all-girls schools as a child. She went to the Graham School near her home from approximately 1912 until 1916. The Graham School focused on helping students learn to think for themselves. Students studied reading, literature, geography, and spelling as well as French, singing, Bible stories, and penmanship.

In December 1916, Grace's parents switched her from the Graham School to Miss Mary Schoonmaker's School. Grace was very active at the new school, playing basketball, water polo, and field hockey. In addition, students at Miss Mary's had to read and report on 20 books each summer. Fortunately, Grace loved to read. She graduated from Miss Mary's in 1923.

The next question for Grace was where to attend college. In reality, she had answered that question years before. Her cousin had graduated from Vassar College when Grace was 15 years

The Murray children grew up in busy New York City, with plenty of museums and concert halls to explore.

old. Grace's mother likewise supported her daughter's interest in the school, a women's college located in Poughkeepsie, New York. Grace took the necessary exams to get into Vassar in the summer of 1923. Yet she failed the Latin exam. The Murray family consulted with Vassar officials, and they decided Grace should wait one year and then reapply. At that time, she was not even 18 years old. In the meantime, she would go back to school.

THREE

COLLEGE STUDENT

In the fall of 1923, Grace entered the Hartridge School in Plainfield, New Jersey, as a boarding student. The Hartridge School was a high school that focused on preparing its students for college, especially Vassar. Vassar was the alma mater of the school's headmistress, Emelyn Hartridge. At Hartridge, young women studied trigonometry, geometry, algebra, English, and US history. They also had their choice of languages to study, including Latin, which was taught by Hartridge. Grace studied Latin and had no problem passing the Vassar entrance exam in that subject the following year.

September 1924 saw Grace moving to New York State's Hudson River Valley to begin her studies at Vassar College. Vassar belongs to a group of women's colleges that are

Grace was a dedicated student while at Vassar College, spending her free time tutoring other students.

Matthew Vassar started construction on Vassar College in 1861.

historically known as the Seven Sisters, though it now admits
men as well. The school welcomed its first students in 1865 with
a mission to offer young women a liberal arts education that was
as good as that of the best colleges for men. It quickly gained a
reputation as a demanding school where women could study
both arts and sciences. Vassar instructors often were leading
scholars in their fields of study. They encouraged their students
to ask questions and think independently. Grace focused her
studies on mathematics and physics. She also studied beginning
sciences, business, and economics.

STUDIES AND ADVENTURES

At Vassar, Grace focused her time and attention on her studies.
She did not engage in student government, nor did she pursue

athletics at the school, even though she continued to spend active summers at the family property in New Hampshire. She had made good grades in high school, and she now earned high marks at Vassar. She was elected to Phi Beta Kappa, the United States' oldest and most prestigious honor society. The Phi Beta Kappa chapter at Vassar was the first one founded at a women's college.

Once during college, Grace treated herself to a special adventure. She noticed a biplane had landed in a field nearby. Grace was excited to discover that one could buy a ride in the

Applied and Theoretical Mathematics

At Vassar, Grace was able to study with top mathematicians. Many of these professors had been trained in Europe, where mathematics instruction tended to focus on how mathematics could be used to solve problems in everyday life. In the United States at the time, the study of math tended to be more pure, or theoretical. This was the study of mathematics for its own sake. Many American scholars even believed applied mathematics was suitable only for those who could not handle the rigor of theoretical mathematics. That started to change when Grace and others began proving the value of applied mathematics in areas such as engineering, business, and computers. One example of how applied mathematics has greatly advanced science is the use of computers and mathematics to create simulations that reduce cost and time for experiments. Decades ago, scientists used giant wind tunnels to examine wind flow over aircraft bodies. Through the use of applied mathematics and computers, scientists are now able to mathematically draw the aircraft on a computer and simulate how the air will flow over the shape of a new aircraft design.

plane. "It had an engine and an open cockpit so you got the full benefit of the wind," Grace recalled of the biplane, which was constructed of wood, linen, and wire. "I squandered all my money—it cost $10—and went up in that plane." Grace's ten-dollar fare was equal to nearly $140 today.[1]

Grace planned to use her education to become a teacher, or possibly an actuary, a person who calculates statistics and risks and usually works in the insurance business. Her younger sister enrolled in Vassar two years later and used her studies to prepare for a career in statistics. It was during her time at Vassar that Grace learned she had a special gift when it came to teaching. She realized she had the ability to take complicated concepts and explain them in terms most everyone could understand. "I have always made the connection between the theoretical—the theory itself—and the reality," she said. "That's the way you explain things."[2]

TUTOR

Grace used that skill to tutor the daughter of a Vassar administrator. The young woman was failing physics until Grace stepped in. Thanks to Grace's help, the woman went from failing the midterm exam to earning an A at the end of the year. The woman later acknowledged Grace's help in a letter she wrote to the Vassar alumnae magazine. "With her help, I suddenly began to understand the approach to science," she wrote in 1996.[3]

Hopper remained a teacher in some capacity throughout the course of her long career.

Following that success, word quickly went around Vassar of Grace's tutoring abilities, and she began assisting more students. A popular story about Grace's teaching skills concerns her technique to explain the concept of displacement. She would have her students go into a bathroom and have one climb into a tub partially filled with water. The students would then note the water level in the tub both before and after the student climbed into it.

Vincent Hopper

Vincent Hopper was the son of a minister. As a student, he was a literary prodigy. He was elected to the honor society Phi Beta Kappa as a junior while studying English at Princeton University. He went on to earn a master's from Princeton and a PhD from Columbia University. In addition to a distinguished teaching career at New York University, he enjoyed success as a literary critic, author, and translator. He died in 1976 from cancer at the age of 69.

It was during her years at Vassar that Grace met the man who would become her husband. Vincent Foster Hopper's family had a summer home in New Hampshire not far from the Murrays'. He also had a car. Grace's sister, Mary, recalled that Vincent would take the Murray girls to the movies.

Sometimes there would be so many people packed into the car that they would spill out onto the running boards. Vincent and Grace got to know each other during several summers. He was studying at Princeton University while Grace was at Vassar. Mary Murray recalled her sister receiving letters from

Vincent while they were dating, all marked by the prestigious Princeton seal.

Grace graduated with honors from Vassar in 1928 with a double major in mathematics and physics. Her accomplishments also earned her a Vassar College Fellowship to pursue a master of arts degree in mathematics at Yale University. Yale, located in New Haven, Connecticut, had been Walter Murray's alma mater. Grace moved to Connecticut and completed the master's degree in 1930, after the United States entered the Great Depression. She and Vincent Hopper were married in June 1930, at the West End Collegiate Church in New York City. They embarked on an eight-week honeymoon in Europe with Grace's family. The newlyweds, along with her parents and her brother Roger and his wife, left New York on a ship bound across the Atlantic. They toured in

Grace at the Vassar Reunion

Grace once commented that most of her classmates at Vassar had few career goals other than to get married. She said she knew of a few classmates who had pursued graduate degrees and become actuaries, as well as two who worked in a lab. The rest, however, had followed the traditional path of marriage and motherhood. At her 50-year Vassar class reunion, Grace said that little had changed. "After I'd been there about twenty minutes, I found myself being very polite to all the nice old ladies."[4] It was Grace's way of saying she was bored.

Stonehenge's stone circle has stood for approximately
4,500 years.

France, England, Wales, and Scotland in the family Buick, driven

by Grace's mother.

Grace was especially enthralled by their visit to Stonehenge,

located on the Salisbury Plain southwest of London. Over the

years, Grace made several visits to the prehistoric remains

of a circle of huge standing stones. No one knows for certain who built the monument or why. Several theories indicate the formation might have served as an early astronomical computer used to predict eclipses or possibly the change of seasons. As for Grace, she had her own changes on the horizon, including a return to the classroom.

FOUR

BACK TO VASSAR

F ollowing the honeymoon, the newlyweds settled in New York City in an apartment on the same street where Hopper had grown up. Her brother and his wife lived nearby, as did her sister and her husband, along with her parents. Vincent, who had just received his master's degree from Princeton, had taken a job teaching English at New York University's School of Commerce. He also was working on a PhD in comparative literature at Columbia University. Hopper returned to Yale to begin work on her PhD in mathematics.

For Hopper, the PhD program at Yale involved working with two professors who were significant influences in her career. One was algebraist Øystein Ore. Hopper described Ore to her sister as a very demanding Scandinavian. She also began

Hopper studied for her PhD degree while teaching mathematics courses at Vassar College.

Teaching Technical Concepts

One of Hopper's favorite "show, don't tell" examples of teaching involved explaining nanoseconds. A nanosecond is one billionth of a second, and computer circuits operate in that amount of time. Hopper knew how hard it is for the average person to visualize how much a billion is. So she carried an 11.8-inch (29.9 cm) piece of wire with her wherever she traveled. The wire represented a nanosecond with the maximum distance that electricity can travel in a billionth of a second.

One of Hopper's favorite nanosecond stories involved an admiral who wanted to know why it took so long to send a message via satellite. Hopper explained to him that there were a great many nanoseconds between where the admiral had sent the message and where the receiving satellite was located high above the Earth.

work with Howard T. Engstrom, whom she continued to have contact with after leaving Yale. As with her Vassar entrance exam, a language issue arose during her doctoral studies. Hopper needed to pass a German language exam, but she did not want to take lessons in German. Her solution was to buy two versions of a single mathematics textbook—one written in German, one in English. Using both books, she taught herself enough German to pass the test and secure her degree.

FROM STUDENT TO TEACHER

Hopper was still a PhD student when she accepted a job teaching mathematics at Vassar in 1931. She began as an assistant in mathematics for an annual salary of $800, which was

Hopper liked to use a wire as a visual aid to explain to students the distance electricity could travel in one nanosecond.

less than $13,000 in today's dollars.[1] As a junior staff member, Hopper was assigned to teach the classes with the largest enrollments and those that no one else wanted to teach. That included calculus, basic trigonometry, and mechanical and architectural drawing.

Ever a dedicated teacher, she found herself challenged with teaching mechanical drawing to a left-handed student. She spent hours figuring out how to reverse T-squares and triangles. She also worked overtime to liven up the classes students dreaded. She engaged her mechanical drawing students by having them create imaginary countries with entire cities and populations. She also drew upon the growing popularity of animated films by having her students draw animations, as well as the informative graphs that were becoming popular in newspapers. In a move that mirrored what she would be doing in the not-too-distant future, she taught her calculus students about ballistics, only she substituted the more exciting idea of rockets instead of the traditional

Language Challenges and Gifts

Hopper acknowledged that she could not learn foreign languages by studying grammar. She also said she could not really speak any language other than English. If she had to understand foreign words, she learned to get by with a dictionary. The ambidextrous Hopper did, however, have a unique talent to impress her students. She could start writing on the blackboard with her left hand in German and then finish what she was writing with her right hand in French.

work in bullets. It was not
long before Hopper's classes
became a popular option for
students in all majors.

Hopper also encouraged
her students to practice
their writing. She would
give lectures on topics in
mathematics and assign the
students to write up the
lecture. She then evaluated
their writing. Many math
students objected to
receiving papers marked up in red in a math course. Yet Hopper
was firm in her belief that writing was an essential skill, and
she knew even math students would not get anywhere in their
careers unless they could communicate clearly.

Curious Learner

One of the perks of teaching at Vassar
was the option to audit other classes.
When a person audits a course, he
or she attends the class and does the
work but does not receive a grade or
credit for the course. Hopper used this
benefit to learn the basics of astronomy,
bacteriology, architecture, and geology,
among other subjects. She said these
additional studies came in handy when
she was working in computers and could
envision how the new technology could
be used to solve problems in multiple
fields of study.

OUTSIDE THE CLASSROOM

As they had in childhood, Hopper and Vincent spent summers
in New Hampshire. In 1932, they bought an old farmhouse with
money received as a wedding gift. The house, plus 60 acres
(24 ha) of land, cost them $450.[2] The farmhouse had no running
water, electricity, or heat, but Hopper and Vincent stayed there
every summer from 1932 to 1941. For fun, the young couple

Hopper's Hobbies

Hopper spent many hours knitting and making rugs for her family members and friends. In later years, she became a collector of books, American and British colonial stamps, dolls, and souvenirs from her many travels. A mathematician at heart, she was attracted to sets and series of things. She belonged to a club for collectors of china and also collected figurines. She also loved to shop, especially for shoes. At the time of her death she had collected more than 3,000 dolls and 10,000 books.

played golf or badminton, and Hopper knitted sweaters and hooked rugs.

Hopper's work at Vassar meant she was working on her Yale dissertation in absentia. She was awarded her PhD in mathematics from Yale in 1934. She wrote her dissertation on "The Irreducibility of Algebraic Equations." She was one of only seven individuals to receive a PhD in mathematics from Yale between 1934 and 1937. Of those seven, Hopper was the only woman.

She continued teaching at Vassar after receiving her PhD, and she eventually became an associate professor there. She had been commuting from New York City in her 1928 Model-A Ford. In 1939, she and Vincent built a house in Poughkeepsie, though Vincent continued to live in New York City during the week because of his job. In 1941, Hopper won a two-year faculty fellowship at Vassar, which meant she could teach half-time and take classes the rest of the time while still receiving her full salary. She chose to exercise the study option by taking graduate courses at New York University's Department of Mathematics. Studying with Richard Courant, she plunged into the calculus of variations and differential geometry, both of which deal with surfaces, planes, and curves. Hopper recalled that she was at times a frustrating student for her mentor. "I kept doing unorthodox things and wanting to tackle unorthodox problems."[3]

PEARL HARBOR

Hopper's life took a dramatic new turn after the events of December 7, 1941. She recalls being in the study of her home in Poughkeepsie with Vincent when they heard about the attack on Pearl Harbor. The United States swiftly entered World War II (1939–1945) and joined forces with the United Kingdom, the Soviet Union, France, and other countries that comprised the Allied forces fighting against Germany, Italy, Japan, and other countries that made up the Axis powers. The reality of living in a nation at war quickly joined another reality the couple had been struggling with for years. Their marriage had been a whirlwind of advanced studies, teaching responsibilities, and hours of commuting. All had taken a toll on the couple's relationship, and they decided to separate at the end of 1941.

After the separation, Hopper continued to split her time between teaching at Vassar and studying at New York University. Her family, meanwhile, did what they could to help

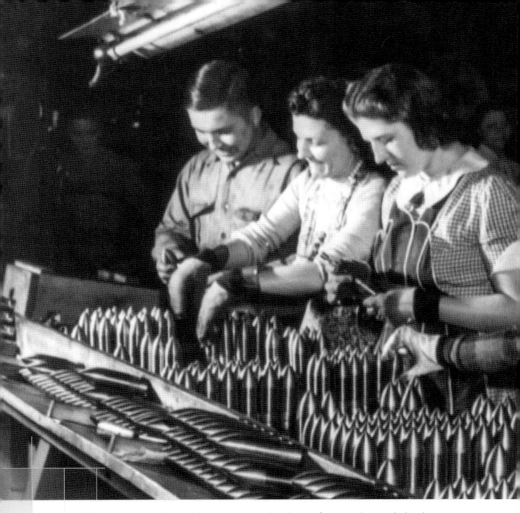

Women work alongside men in an aluminum factory that switched over to manufacturing ammunition during the war.

the war effort. Her brother volunteered for the army. Her father served on the Selective Service Board, which handled drafting men to fight in the military, and her mother served on a local rationing board, which administered stamps that allowed civilians to purchase limited quantities of certain foods and other goods. Hopper's sister worked for General Electric, running the

company's nursery so the women working there could make fuses for bombs. Hopper, too, wanted to do something to help the war effort, but women were only allowed in very selective, noncombatant military roles. Changing that would require an act of Congress.

FIVE

IN THE NAVY

In July 1942, Congress authorized the Navy Women's Reserve, the World War II women's branch of the US Naval Reserve. This led to the creation of the WAVES, or Women Accepted for Volunteer Emergency Services. Acceptance into the WAVES program came with several restrictions. Women were only allowed to serve as emergency personnel, and they could only sign on for the duration of the war, plus another six months. In addition, women were limited to jobs that kept them within the United States. Hopper sought a slot in the program. She said she chose the navy because of her great-grandfather Rear Admiral John H. Russell. As it turned out, getting into the navy was not easy. Hopper failed the physical exam because she was five feet six inches (1.7 m) tall and weighed 105 pounds (47.6 kg).

Hopper graduated first in her class from Naval Reserve Midshipmen's School at Smith College in Northampton, Massachusetts, in 1944.

According to navy guidelines, at that height she needed to weigh at least 121 pounds (54.9 kg). Hopper made it clear to the navy that she was lean and tough, and she did not need to weigh any more than 105 pounds.

Another barrier to Hopper's navy plans was her profession. Mathematics was viewed as an important element of the war effort, so anyone teaching math had to get a special authorization to do something different. Hopper had to apply for the WAVES and apply to Vassar for permission to join the WAVES. As she waited for her approvals, she took

Wartime Code Cracking in the US Navy

During World War II, Allied forces sought to break the secret communication codes used by Nazi forces. The US Navy assembled a group of mathematicians to crack enemy codes at the Naval Communications Annex in Washington, DC.

In 1942, the navy joined with the National Cash Register Company (NCR) to create a code-breaking machine. The result was the Bombe machine, which was created to decode messages created by the German Enigma machine. It required the efforts of 600 WAVES working at the NCR facility in Ohio, along with 100 navy officers and enlisted men, plus a civilian workforce, to build the first Bombe machines. Security on the project was so tight that each WAVES member had instructions only for the part of the machine on which she was working. It was not until the WAVES were transferred to Washington, DC, that any of them saw a completed machine.

The Bombe dramatically increased the navy's ability to decipher messages. At the beginning of 1943, it took approximately 600 hours to decipher a single message. The Bombe slashed that time to 18 hours.

a job at Barnard College teaching women who had enrolled in war preparedness courses. In late 1943, she received both an approval from Vassar and a waiver from the navy for the weight requirement. She was sworn into the US Navy in December 1943.

AT HOME IN THE WAVES

Hopper's next stop was WAVES officer training at the Naval Reserve Midshipmen's School at Smith College in Massachusetts. She received 60 days of training. She later characterized the training as "Thirty days to learn how to take orders, and thirty days to learn how to give orders."[1] The training included teaching Hopper and the other recruits how to compose military letters and reports, recognize ships and aircraft, and march in formation. Hopper realized she enjoyed the marching drills as she was quite good at them, and they reminded her of dancing. Perhaps more importantly, Hopper learned the lingo of the navy. "We had to have good enough sense to talk about the deck and the overhead and not the floor and the ceiling," she said.[2]

One area where she did struggle was navy protocol. Standard navy protocol meant junior officers always let their superior officers enter a room first. As a woman in the navy, this sometimes backfired. "I had the darndest time trying to let admirals go through doors ahead of me and they tried to treat

Women Mathematicians in World War II

Hopper was just one of the women mathematicians who served their country during World War II. In 1942, hundreds of women were employed using mechanical desk calculators to create ballistics tables for use by gunners on the battlefield. Some of them worked at the Moore School of Electrical Engineering at the University of Pennsylvania in Philadelphia. Mary Mauchly was one of them, and her husband, John, a professor there, decided to design a machine that could do the same task. He began work on the ENIAC (Electronic Numerical Integrator and Computer). While the ENIAC was not completed until after World War II, six of its initial programmers were women: Kay McNulty, Frances Bilas, Betty Jean Jennings, Elizabeth Snyder, Ruth Lichterman, and Marlyn Wescoff.

me like a lady and get me through the door first and we usually ended up going through together, which was bad," she recalled.[3]

At age 37, Hopper was older than most of the other recruits. She also was unusual in that she was married and had no children. Most of her fellow volunteers were young, single women, and some of them had been her students at either Barnard or Vassar. For Hopper, the navy meant an easier, less complicated life. Her daily routines were prescribed. There was no commuting or juggling of jobs with studies and writing papers or taking care of a household.

SETTLING IN

Hopper said of her navy years that she took to her military service "like a featherbed and gained weight and had a perfectly heavenly time."[4] She graduated at the head of her 800-member class on June 27, 1944, when she was commissioned as, or officially given the title of, a lieutenant, junior grade, rising from the entry-level rank of ensign.

Meanwhile, the navy had taken over a computer at Harvard University. The Bureau of Ordnance Computation Project at Harvard was under the direction of Navy Commander Howard Aiken. Aiken promptly informed the navy that he needed more mathematicians for his project. When he learned there was a WAVES member with a PhD in mathematics, he had asked for Hopper to be assigned to him immediately, instead of going through training. The navy ignored his request, and Hopper arrived two months later than Aiken had wanted, on July 2, 1944.

Hopper had no idea what she would be doing when she walked into the door of the Cruft Laboratory. She quickly found out. Aiken pointed to the Mark I and said, "That's a computing engine. I would be delighted to have the coefficients for the interpolation of the

The Path to the Harvard Lab

Hopper believed her navy assignment would be with her former Yale instructor Howard Engstrom, who was leading the navy's Communications Supplementary Activity in Washington, DC. She was surprised to find out she was being sent to Harvard instead. In filling out her application for the navy, Hopper had noted a course in the solution of partial differential equations that she had taken with Richard Courant during her faculty fellowship at New York University. That background made her a fit for Commander Aiken, who was seeking mathematicians with experience in finite differences.

arc tangents by next Thursday."[5] Hopper had joined a small team that was programming the first modern computer, the Mark I. The Mark I, also called the Automatic Sequence Controlled Calculator, had begun some six years earlier. It was a joint project of Aiken, who was an associate professor of applied mathematics at Harvard, and a group of engineers from International Business Machines (IBM). The Mark I took up residence at Harvard in the summer of 1944. It was 51 feet

The Harvard Mark I, or Automatic Sequence Controlled Calculator, was housed in a large room on the campus of Harvard University in Cambridge, Massachusetts.

(15.5 m) long, 8 feet (2.4 m) high and weighed nearly 9,500 pounds (4,300 kg).[6] In addition to Hopper, Navy Second Lieutenants Robert Campbell and Richard Bloch also were assigned to program the Mark I. Later, another WAVES member, Ruth Brendel, joined the team.

QUICK STUDY

Campbell later recalled that he and Bloch had heard

Commander Howard Aiken

Commander Howard Hathaway Aiken was an associate professor of applied mathematics at Harvard before being called to active duty in the navy in 1941. His hard-driving personality was formed early, when he became responsible for his mother after forcing his alcoholic father out of the house with a fireplace poker at age 12. Aiken worked for a utility company while putting himself through school for an engineering degree and later a PhD in physics. Aiken became a full professor at Harvard in 1946 and retired from the university in 1961. He had a successful consulting business after retirement and died in 1973.

they would be joined by an "old lady school teacher" from Vassar.[7] They quickly learned that Hopper was anything but that. Campbell had to show her how the Mark I operated, but Hopper was a quick study, asking lots of questions. Bloch recalled being impressed at how quickly Hopper caught on to the applied mathematics tasks of the Mark I as opposed to the theoretical mathematics focus of her teaching career.

In Hopper's case, the applied mathematics had to do with how bullets fired out of shipboard guns. Gun operators had long considered factors such as wind, air temperature,

Joking Around

Hopper used practical jokes and humor to help cut the tension in the Harvard computer lab, which was run by Howard Aiken, a strict disciplinarian. Once she faked the overnight report of the Mark I's activities to make it look as though nothing had happened. An angry Aiken interrogated the staff members, who were puzzled by his questions. When he looked at the log again, it had been changed to reflect a normal routine. He realized he'd been the target of a practical joke and laughed along with everyone else.

and shell weight when determining where to aim their guns. During World War I, navy gunners had a simple device they called the Baby Ford that helped them calculate range rate, bearing rate, and present range for their guns, which are all the measurements and numbers necessary to accurately fire the weapons.

In World War II, the shells became better, with higher explosive capacity and different gunpowder. Their simple machine was no longer sufficient.

Hopper recalled of the time, "There was a rush on everything, and we didn't realize what was really happening. All of a sudden we had self-propelled rockets, and we had to compute where they were going and what they were going to do."[8] In addition, Hopper's team used the Mark I to determine how much area was covered by a mine-sweeping detector towed behind a ship. Those calculations helped the navy better place its underwater mines.

Howard Aiken, *seated, left,* worked with a team of mathematicians, including Hopper, from 1939 to 1944 developing the Harvard Mark I calculator.

53

AGAINST THE CLOCK, AROUND THE CLOCK

The next two years saw Hopper and the Harvard team working feverishly, sometimes nonstop. Hopper recalled how she might be at the computer laboratory around the clock if the Mark I was running one of her programs. "I always loved a good gadget," she said later of the Mark I. "When I met Mark I, it was the biggest fanciest gadget I'd ever seen."[1] Demand for the Mark I was substantial. During the war, it ran 24 hours a day, seven days a week.

Her natural communications skills also came into play. At midshipmen's school, she had learned the language of the navy. Now she had to learn the language of oceanography, ballistics, and detonators. "We had to learn their vocabularies in order to be able to run their problems," she recalled. "I could

Hopper and Aiken inspect parts of an early calculating machine.

The Manhattan Project

Hopper had been at Harvard two months when a new guest arrived with a special project for the Mark I. John von Neumann was a mathematician and a specialist in supersonic and turbulent fluid flows. He was consulting with both the army and the navy and had found himself staring down a hard-to-solve equation. Neumann worked with Hopper and Bloch to program the problem for the Mark I, and Neumann used the results from that work to complete his analysis for the top-secret Manhattan Project. It was not until nearly a year later when the atomic bomb was dropped on Hiroshima and Nagasaki that Hopper and Bloch realized what they had been working on.

switch my vocabulary and speak highly technical for the programmers, and then tell the same things to the managers a few hours later with a totally different vocabulary," she said.[2]

That skill also came in handy when it came to a special assignment from Aiken. Among Hopper's duties with the Mark I was creating a manual for how to use it. Hopper recalled how Aiken assigned her to write the technical documentation for the massive machine. "He told me he wanted me to write a book," Hopper recalled. "I said I couldn't write a book. He said I was in the navy now; so I wrote a book."[3] Hopper's *A Manual of Operation for the Automatic Sequence Controlled Calculator* included not only photographs and schematic diagrams of the Mark I and detailed directions for how to work with punched cards, but also literary and humorous quotes. By the time Hopper finished the manual, World War II was nearly at an end.

Hopper assists with checking the sequence mechanism on the Mark I calculator.

PERSONAL CROSSROADS

Hopper now had a decision to make. She did not want to return to the classroom at Vassar. In addition, she and Vincent had officially divorced in 1945, a stressful issue for her. Divorce was still viewed as unacceptable at that time. Hopper did not change her name, did not speak of the divorce, and did not like others to do so, either. Even the *New York Times* inaccurately reported that she had been widowed, and she chose not to correct the article.

Bugs in the System

Hopper often is credited with coining the term *debugging* in the computer world. The term stemmed from a time when she was working on the Mark II and it suddenly stopped. Hopper and her team traced the problem to a moth that had gotten caught in one of the computer's relays, or switches. "We got a pair of tweezers," Hopper recalled. "Very carefully we took the moth out of the relay, put it in the logbook, and then put scotch tape over it."[4] She added that the team turned the incident into an ongoing joke. "From then on, if we weren't making any numbers, we told . . . Aiken that we were debugging the computer."[5]

In the end, Hopper decided instead on a career in the navy, as that body was now allowing women to take up active duty. There was one problem—she was 40 years old, and the navy considered her too old for service. Her only option was to remain in the Naval Reserve and continue working with the Mark I as its usage was expanded from military operations to commercial ones.

Commander Aiken secured Hopper a position as a Harvard research associate, and Hopper continued as one of the few programmers who saw a future for computers outside of the military and academic institutions.

She also joined former teammates Bloch and Campbell to program the Mark I's successor, the Mark II. The Mark II was five times faster than its predecessor. Taking up approximately 4,000 square feet (370 sq m) of space, it used vacuum tubes and magnetic tape. Vacuum tubes that did not have moving parts and relied on electricity were more reliable than computers constructed of moving mechanical relays. These could jam or break down.

Hopper worked on the Mark II until 1948, when the Mark III computer took its place. It was during that time that Hopper and her teammates began keeping a notebook of pieces of code that they had already tested. One example might be the code to do the math to find geometric calculations, such as a cosine or arctangent. They called these instructions subroutines and referred to their notebooks to place the subroutines in new programs they were working on that involved those same functions.

Hopper's computer "bug" in the logbook under scotch tape

59

SCIENCE
SPOTLIGHT

DEBUGGING

Debugging is an important part of software development that ensures the software functions as it should. Debugging involves multiple steps designed to identify problems, determine what is causing the problems, and either fix the problems or find ways to work around them. The fix or work-around is then tested, and the process may be repeated depending on the results. Debugging typically involves correcting coding errors. Today's software engineers have a variety of tools to assist in the debugging process, including unit testing, code review, and pair programming. Unit testing allows software developers to independently examine the smallest testable parts of an application, which are called units. Code review involves gathering the authors of code, other reviewers, and sometimes quality assurance testers together to review code to find and fix errors prior to including the code in a larger program. Pair programming involves enlisting two different developers to work on a single computer—presumably testing the theory that two heads are better than one.

Women in Postwar Computing

Hopper and the other female mathematicians pressed into computer service during the war had a slight career advantage in the postwar United States because they were already working in the field. That advantage remained even as men began returning from the battlefields. But soon many former servicemen took advantage of the G.I. Bill, which provided educational money to military personnel, to attend college. Women's advantage in computers quickly faded as the G.I. Bill students became employees. Employers tended to hire newly graduated men instead of experienced women.

Hopper never stopped encouraging women to seek careers in computers. Despite her efforts, a gender gap developed that continues to this day. In 1960 and in 1990, women represented approximately 35 percent of computing professionals. By 2013, it had dropped to 26 percent.[6] One theory for this gap involves the advent of personal computers. In the mid-1980s, the marketing of computers focused on games targeting men and boys. Some researchers believe this created a cultural bias in computers that favors men over women.

CHOOSING EMCC

Hopper's contract with Harvard ended in 1949. She began job hunting and ended up with two offers. She elected to take the offer from start-up Eckert-Mauchly Computer Corporation, or EMCC. Hopper believed EMCC was closer to having the kind of computer she wanted to work on. Plus, it was in Philadelphia, Pennsylvania, which was closer to her family in New York than the other job offer she received.

Alcohol and Depression

Hopper's years at Harvard and EMCC showcased her talent for innovation and her impressive technical skills. The stress of those positions also created challenges in her personal life. It led to Hopper drinking too much alcohol on the weekends. Sometimes she even drank during the workday. Particularly bad episodes could keep her at a barely functional level at the office. On two occasions, it is believed she even contemplated suicide. These issues continued into her employment at EMCC, where she was arrested for drunk and disorderly conduct in November 1949. Fortunately for Hopper, she had friends and family to help her rally and seek treatment.

EMCC presented Hopper with challenges very different from those of the Harvard lab. As EMCC was a start-up company, Hopper had to deal with a host of uncertainties. Before EMCC was acquired by Remington Rand, she and others even accepted salary decreases so the company could purchase supplies to keep the UNIVAC program going. The acquisition meant Hopper's work could continue, from the groundbreaking UNIVAC on to her breakthrough compiler, the A-0 compiler. The UNIVAC project also allowed her to see her vision of computers in business take root. Perhaps most importantly, EMCC allowed Hopper's leadership to shine. Her management experience from Harvard and years in the Vassar classroom allowed her to manage projects efficiently while helping younger team members grow.

The advances Hopper and her colleagues made at the Harvard University Aiken Computation Lab helped revolutionize the computer.

Hopper also continued writing about the field, including the future, with amazingly accurate results. She correctly predicted that software, not hardware, would become the more expensive component of computer systems because of the time it takes to develop. Her writing also was the first to refer to subroutines, formula translators (compilers that could translate mathematical formulas into computer code), and code optimization (techniques to make computer code as fast and efficient as possible). All would become standard tools and techniques for the industry.

Vacuum tubes, such as these from the 1950s, controlled the flow of electrons and greatly increased the reliability and processing capabilities of computers.

SCIENCE
SPOTLIGHT

DELAY-LINE MEMORY

The UNIVAC I, for which Hopper wrote her first compiler, featured one of the first successful operating memories for a computer. An operating memory provided internal storage for information instead of relying solely on information as it was input. The technology it used was called a mercury delay line. EMCC cofounder J. Presper Eckert developed the mercury delay line during World War II to improve radar function.

In the UNIVAC I, this memory was a series of 18 metal tanks, with each tank containing a long, narrow glass tube filled with mercury. Data in the form of electrical pulses was compressed down to sound waves and sent through the mercury-filled tubes, which slowed it down. At the other end, the signal was amplified and bounced back to the beginning of the tube, a process which could go on indefinitely. The mercury in the tubes meant that hundreds of pulses of data could be sent in a single tube and bounce back and forth in stored memory until they were needed. The primary advantage of the technology was its ability to store and access information at high speeds. One drawback was that the information could only be accessed sequentially, or in the order it was stored.

ENTER COBOL

In 1953, Hopper presented Remington Rand management with a proposal suggesting that mathematical problems could be presented to a computer in mathematical notation and that business problems should be written in English. "There are a lot of people who don't get along with symbols, so they use words," she remarked. "As far as I'm concerned, a word is a symbol, it's just a little bit longer. There's no difference between the word a-d-d and the plus sign, so why not write it in English?"[1] Her request for funding for the project was denied, because no one believed a computer could understand English words. As she had before, Hopper continued to work on her project quietly and on her own. "When you have a good idea and you've tried it and you know it's going to work, go ahead and do it," she would

In 1959, Hopper demonstrates COBOL, a user-friendly computer language she helped develop.

tell audiences years later. "Because it's much easier to apologize afterwards than it is to get permission."[2]

By early 1955, Hopper had a demonstration program that proved her idea was workable. She gathered her company's top management in a room and showed them how she could assign a computer to create a pricing and inventory file using instructions in English. She then instructed the computer to do the same work in both French and German.

The Remington Rand UNIVAC computer had its own data processing room.

Members of the management team became angered when they thought Hopper was suggesting the computer would be programmed in French or German. It took Hopper another four months to convince them that the UNIVAC would only be programmed in English. The foreign languages had simply been to prove the concept. Once she had made that point clear, her work was funded, and she and her team created the B-0 compiler, which later became known as FLOW-MATIC. She summed up the project simply as "We figured we would make it easy for people."[3]

FLOW-MATIC changed the course of computer programming. Future compilers would follow the pattern it established. That reality, however, was lost on the management of Hopper's company, now Sperry Rand after a 1955 merger with Sperry. Hopper found herself going directly to the company's customers to sell the value of the compiler, because her company's own management would not. She came up with the term *layette* to describe the compiler, as something to be sold along with the computer itself. Eventually the term was changed to *software*. In time, even Sperry Rand management could not ignore the praise for FLOW-MATIC coming from its customers. Suddenly, Hopper had funding and support. By 1957, she also had a new project.

COBOL and Y2K

The late 1990s brought increasing worry about the "Y2K bug." This was a feature in many software programs, including COBOL, that allowed dates to be entered with six digits—two for the day, two for the month, and two for the year. As the year 2000 approached, many in the industry were concerned that programs might read the year entry 00 as 1900 instead of 2000. Programmers were able to fix Y2K issues, but the question remained as to why the systems had been set up that way in the first place. Robert Bemer, who wrote much of the COBOL language while at IBM, said the bug was not the fault of any one person, including Hopper. In fact, a fix for the Y2K "bug" was already available as early as the 1950s.

CREATING A COMMON LANGUAGE

The late 1950s saw three major computer languages battling it out for supremacy in the still-new sector. There was Hopper's FLOW-MATIC, IBM's FORTRAN and Massachusetts Institute of Technology's (MIT's) Automatically Programmed Tools, or APT. The question arose of how to develop a common business language. In April 1959, Hopper joined in those discussions under the Conference on Data System Languages. By June 1960, the group had agreed on common business-oriented language, or COBOL, as the standard language for business programming. It was based more on FLOW-MATIC than the other commonly used languages. Following development of a COBOL compiler, the new language was tested on both a UNIVAC II from Remington Rand and an RCA 501 from RCA. That successful test run demonstrated that a single data-processing language could be used on different computers created by different manufacturers.

COBOL went on to become one of the world's most popular programming languages and a standard for mainframe computers. Hopper's former colleague, Robert Campbell, credited that to Hopper. "Grace would get a problem and not let go of it until it was solved," he said. "I think it was this quality that allowed her to complete her work on COBOL." Former colleague Richard Bloch added, "Grace was not the only one who was working on the idea of compilers, but she probably was the one who pushed the hardest . . . that was the kind of person she was, she never gave up."[4]

Sperry Rand and IBM

Sperry Rand's computers were powerful, but they were expensive. Its UNIVAC 1100 mainframe computer featured 131 kilobytes of core memory and sold for $823,000.[5] At that same time, a new Ford Mustang car cost approximately $3,000. Despite its advanced technology, Sperry Rand ultimately lost its bid to dominate the mainframe industry, and IBM triumphed. Sperry Rand eventually merged with competitor Burroughs in 1986 to become Unisys, an information technology company specializing in software.

In August 1961, Hopper was promoted to director of research and systems and programming for the Remington Rand Division of Sperry Rand. In 1964, she was appointed senior staff scientist at the company's UNIVAC division. The new role gave her the opportunity to travel widely, discussing UNIVAC issues in Europe and Japan as well as around the United States and Canada. The duties kept Hopper busy, yet she had concerns about her future with the company. At age 60, she knew she could stay with Sperry Rand until at least age 65. Yet she was already scouting around for other opportunities. One option was to go into civil service, which includes government agencies outside of the armed services, where she could work until age 70. "I will do almost anything to stay with the computers," she said in 1966 at the age of 60. "The field is still critically shorthanded. Of course, I hope the price will come down some day so I can have a computer of my own."[6]

Compilers—and How a Game Inspired Them

Among Hopper's software innovations was a concept known as jumping. It meant programmers could "jump" forward in a program to a section that had not yet been written. In a 1989 interview, Hopper explained how the idea for the jump technique was inspired by her experiences playing basketball as a schoolgirl.

When Hopper was a girl, women's basketball rules limited players to one dribble, after which the ball had to be passed. A player seeking to score a basket might need to pass the ball to a teammate, then run to a spot from which she could shoot a basket and wait for a teammate to pass her the ball. Similarly, Hopper set up a "neutral corner" of memory at the bottom of a program. If she needed to jump forward in a program, she could jump to the neutral corner, place a reminder, and jump to where she wanted to go later in the program. The note in the "neutral corner" served as a reminder to the computer that it needed to check for instructions as each routine was assembled in the program, essentially passing the ball back out of the corner to where it was needed.

BACK IN UNIFORM

In 1966, Hopper received a letter from the navy informing her that she had served more than 23 years and she should retire. She had been in the Naval Reserves since being released from active duty in 1946. In 1952, she had been promoted to lieutenant commander, then to commander in 1957. She had been a consistent contributor over the years, helping the navy with computer installations. The navy in turn had written her glowing recommendations and tracked her accomplishments in the corporate sector. Yet she did as instructed and filled out her retirement forms, leaving the reserves on December 31, 1966.

The XE6 Hopper

Hopper correctly predicted that smaller computers would become the tools of choice for most computing jobs. Yet there remains a need for powerful mainframe supercomputers, particularly for science and engineering projects involving large databases or significant computations. The National Energy Research Scientific Computing Center (NERSC) is the primary scientific computing facility serving those needs in the United States. In 2010, NERSC announced its new Cray XE6 supercomputer, named Hopper in her honor. The machine was used to help scientists working with the Planck space telescope in their search for the oldest light in the universe. The Planck had recorded approximately one trillion observations of one billion points in the sky. The computations needed for scientists to understand what those observations meant required more than ten million processor-hours on the Hopper. Thanks to the Hopper's tens of thousands of processors, the Planck analysis codes took only a few weeks to complete. In November 2010, Hopper ranked number five on the Top 500 Supercomputer list. The unit was retired in December 2015.

"It was the saddest day of my life," Hopper said.[7] She would later say that whenever she had hit a wall in her corporate career, it was the navy that would send her an assignment to energize her again. She also believed that in her later years, the navy responded more positively to her work than private industry.

Hopper's retirement ended up being short-lived. The navy called her back for a temporary active-duty post in August 1967. Thanks in part to Hopper's influence, the navy had been an early adopter of COBOL. Now, officials needed her to get COBOL better integrated into their operations and to train other personnel how to work with it. Hopper secured a military leave from Sperry Rand and headed to the Pentagon.

Commander Hopper's retirement from the navy lasted seven months before she was called back into service.

GAME
CHANGER

EQUAL OPPORTUNITIES FOR MEN AND WOMEN IN COMPUTERS

Hopper became a symbol of women in computers and maintained throughout her life that men and women shared equal opportunities in the field. She referred to computers as "just another tool, like a wrench or a potato masher."[8] She said women around the nation handled computers every day, only they were called toasters, refrigerators, or thermostats. Even recipes, she said, were like technical flowcharts in that they specified a series of instructions. She said if there was any blame to be placed, it should be on the people who advertised computers as something mysterious when she saw them "as simple as an abacus."[9]

Hopper attributed her success to hard work, yet she also made many personal accommodations. From forgoing having children to logging long hours, Hopper made the personal sacrifices that were required of working women in her era. She also combined her natural sense of humor with an ability to lead her team in whatever needed to be done to achieve the objective.

Computer technician Joyce Cade assists with the installation of a UNIVAC computer at the US Census Bureau in 1954.

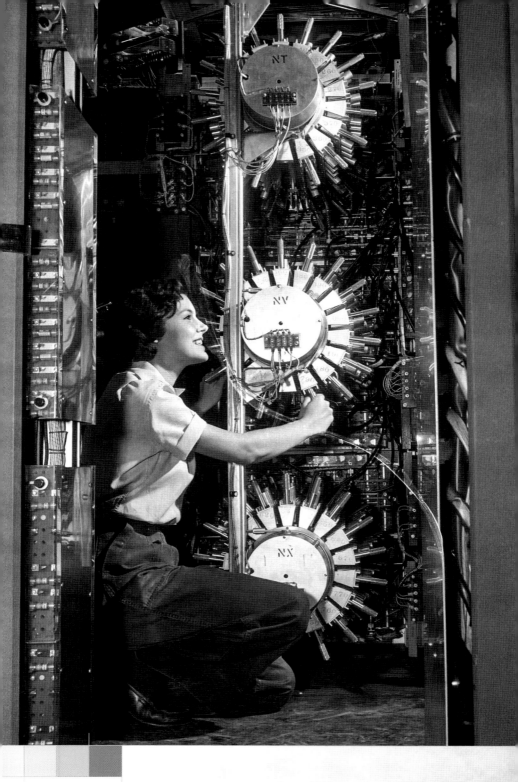

EIGHT

AT THE PENTAGON

O ne of Hopper's first assignments at the Pentagon was a familiar one—write another book. She and her team produced *The Fundamentals of COBOL* to help standardize use of that programming language throughout the navy. Eventually, she helped standardize it throughout the entire US Department of Defense. At the same time, she brought her unconventional thinking into an organization that prided itself on doing things the same way it always had. Hopper believed quite the opposite. She even had a clock in her office that ran counterclockwise. It was a reminder that there was more than one way to do any job. She also had a Jolly Roger flag, the famous pirate flag depicting a skull and crossbones, in her office. That flag was a reminder of the raids she and her team would carry out to

Hopper challenged convention and believed there was more than one way to get a job done.

get the supplies they needed from other military divisions—sometimes in the middle of the night.

Predicting the Future

In 1947, Howard Aiken was quoted as saying, "Only six electronic digital computers would be required to satisfy the computing needs of the entire United States."[1] In contrast, Hopper was among the first to see a much broader application of computers to society. As early as 1953, she was writing about how a compiler would make programming, and thus computers, accessible to more people. She was among the first to support the use of microcomputers and was an early advocate of networking specialized machines together rather than using mainframes.

Hopper's six-month assignment turned into another 19 years with the navy. The navy's success with computers was forcing other parts of the Defense Department to adopt them as well. In 1969, Hopper's peers recognized her for her contributions to COBOL with the first Computer Sciences Man of the Year award, given by the Data Processing Management Association. She continued to renew her leave from Sperry Rand until 1971 when she reached the mandatory retirement age of 65. That same year, Sperry Rand created the Grace Murray Hopper Award in her honor. The award recognizes an outstanding young person working in computers who has made a significant contribution to the field in either a technical or service capacity.

In the navy, many of Hopper's projects increased efficiencies. The United States became involved in active combat in the Vietnam War (1954–1975) in 1965 and deployed 2.7 million troops to Vietnam.[2] As the United States became more involved in Vietnam, Hopper worked with the navy's supply and logistics group to use computers to reduce the labor needed to supply navy personnel in the conflict. In 1967, this change allowed the Naval Supply Center in Oakland, California, to provide forces in Vietnam with twice as many supplies as in the Korean War in 1952, using less than half the personnel.

The implementation of computers at the Naval Supply Center in Oakland allowed the military to resupply troops in Vietnam much faster.

ON THE ROAD

Hopper also began a heavy schedule of speaking engagements on behalf of the navy. She met with other officers to urge them to run computers. She helped train personnel to work with COBOL. She also spoke publicly about computers even as she continued to write articles within the field of computer science. In a speech in Canada in 1973, Hopper suggested that smaller computers could one day take some of the load off of what she referred to as "mainframe dinosaurs."[3] Among her favorite audiences to address were young people at universities as well as corporations and the military. She urged them to consider using computers in whatever field they decided to enter. She also encouraged them to think differently and challenge things

Working with Young People

Hopper had a passion for leading people to realize their full potential. She credits her experience at midshipmen's school for teaching her about leadership. "It's a two-way street," she said. "It's loyalty up and loyalty down. Respect for your superior—keep him informed of what you're up to, make suggestions. Superior, take care of your crew, listen to them, pat 'em on the back when they do a good job."[4] Hopper especially liked working with her youngest and least-experienced crew members, giving them the hardest technical challenges to solve because they did not know they could not be done.

As she did with her students at Vassar, Hopper coached her young employees in industry and the navy to communicate and present themselves well. She was known to keep a coffee can on her desk. Every time one of her crew said "you know" while reporting to her, he or she had to put a quarter in the can. Eventually, the employee would kick the habit.

that had always been done in the same way.

Hopper was also instrumental in coaching her younger colleagues. Many went on to enjoy successful careers in the private sector after working under her supervision. Hopper also made sure that her department had its share of fun. Its offices were located in the subbasement of the Pentagon and had no natural light. That meant they were plunged into darkness whenever the electricity went out. One day Hopper showed up for work with a miner's hat and light as a joke.

Traveling thousands of miles a year, Hopper became a familiar figure to many both at the Pentagon and within the industry. She always wore her navy uniform, which one time caused a couple of people to believe she was a security guard. Other times fellow travelers mistook her for a flight attendant and asked about airline schedules. She also amused audiences with the tale of going through customs and immigration in Toronto, Canada. An officer questioned who she was, and she

The Navy's Best Recruiter

The navy benefited from Hopper's talents in ways beyond her computer expertise. Hopper's position as a high-ranking female officer in her 70s with a quick wit and an arsenal of one-liners made her a favorite interview for reporters and a perfect opportunity for the navy to gain positive publicity. She had a way of public speaking that made everyone in the audience feel as though they were simply having a chat with her. Rarely did she carry notes, and even when she did she seldom used them. Some people speculated that Hopper was in fact the top recruiter for the navy.

told him she was with the navy. He replied, "You must be the oldest thing they've got."[5]

She attempted to retire from the navy again in 1971 at age 65, but that, too, was short-lived. In August 1973, she was promoted to captain. The approval for the promotion required an act of Congress, since she was too old for a regular promotion. She joked that her promotion likely was because of her heavy schedule of speaking engagements. She said she suspected the navy thought she should have "enough ribbons to look impressive."[6] That same year, she became the first woman ever to be named a Distinguished Fellow of the British Computer Society.

From 1973 to 1978, Hopper traveled approximately 300 days out of each year. In addition to her navy duties, she had been named a professorial lecturer at the George Washington University and consistently taught there one evening a week. She also collaborated

Rocking the Navy Boat

Hopper became known for an ability to cut through the navy's red tape to do what she felt was right. In a 1972 interview, she told of a time when a group of people in the navy were urging that online minicomputers be put on board ships to use for administrative tasks. Another group argued against this. The two groups traded memos on their opposing positions for three years with no agreement. Finally, Hopper suggested that the admiral overseeing the project add up the cost in time and money that the two teams had spent on their correspondence. She suggested it would be cheaper to try using the microcomputer on the ship and evaluate how it worked than it was to continue the war of memos. The admiral agreed and ordered the test of the onboard computer.

on a college textbook called *Understanding Computers* that explained computer theory and history in relatable terms.

MOVING TO NAVDAC

In 1977, the navy created the Naval Data Automation Command, or NAVDAC. Hopper was one of five people named as special staff in the new department. Specifically, her job was to stay up-to-date on what was happening in computer science in the public and private sectors and advise the navy on which, if any, new technologies the navy should adopt. One of her suggestions was to adopt a fleet-wide tactical data system for nuclear submarines. The tactical data system was a computerized information-processing system that was used in combat ships. Her recommendation resulted in a Meritorious Service Medal.

Hopper used her teaching skills to connect with younger employees and navy personnel.

FUTURE
TECH

GOOGLE VS. THE GO MASTER

Throughout her career, Hopper endeavored to make programming computers easier and faster. She created shortcuts that could be put in place to make computers more uniform and lessen the manual input work required of the programmers. Eventually, computer programs would become so advanced, they would seem to outthink the user.

Go is an ancient Chinese game of strategy involving the placement of black and white stones on a 19 × 19 grid. The goal of each go player is to surround the opponent's stones with his or her own stones. Once encircled, or captured, the stone is removed from the board and play continues until only one color of stone remains. In March 2016, one of the modern masters of the game, Lee Sedol, lost four games of go in a highly publicized match against his opponent. The event was remarkable in that Sedol's opponent, AlphaGo, was not human.

AlphaGo, acquired by Google in 2014, is the brainchild of artificial intelligence pioneer Demis Hassabis. Hassabis "trained" AlphaGo for the tournament by exposing it to previously played games of professional go players. In addition, AlphaGo played millions of games itself, learning from each one. It also computed

Professional go player Lee Sedol looks back at the go match he lost to AlphaGo.

how likely any given board position was to lead to a win by using 30 million self-generated positions.

AlphaGo's talents have many potential applications beyond besting go masters. Many everyday challenges involve trial and error, from diagnosing tricky diseases to fighting wars against unpredictable enemies. The learning algorithms such as those being honed by AlphaGo have the potential to help humans in these areas and more.

CHAPTER
NINE

REAR ADMIRAL HOPPER

In a December 1983 ceremony, the 77-year-old Hopper was promoted from captain to commodore. The ceremony involved President Ronald Reagan. Later, Hopper recounted a story from the ceremony. "When I first met him, I looked him in the eye and said, 'Mr. President, sir, I'm older than you are.' And you know what? That great big guy giggled! We got along great."[1] Two years later, Hopper's rank was renamed rear admiral, lower half, again by President Reagan. Hopper was the oldest active-duty officer since the retirement of Naval Admiral Hyman J. Rickover, who had served 63 years of active-duty service with the navy.

The promotion brought new attention to Hopper, along with new requests for speaking engagements and additional

Throughout the span of her 43-year naval career, Hopper was praised for her achievements and contributions to the world of computers.

Rear Admiral

In December 1983, Hopper was promoted to commodore, a rank that the navy replaced in 1985 with the designation of rear admiral, lower half. Rear admiral is a one-star flag officer rank in the navy and is equivalent to a brigadier general in the other branches of the armed forces. Promotion to a rear admiral is very selective, as the navy can only have 162 active-duty flag officers at any one time. Both the president and the US Senate must approve a candidate before he or she can receive the rank. As a flag officer, a rear admiral typically commands a small flotilla of ships and may fly the rear admiral's blue-with-white-star pennant over any base or ship upon which he or she is serving.

honors and awards. In 1984 alone, she received 17 awards, including induction into the Engineering and Science Hall of Fame. The event also increased the number of people contacting her for help and advice. The correspondence became so great that Hopper was forced to accept an assistant.

Hopper hated to turn anyone down if they needed help or a speaker. Yet by 1986, she was 79 years old and beginning to travel less. Navy leaders agreed that she should retire, but no one wanted to break the news to her. In the end, Admiral Paul Sutherland had to take Hopper aside and inform her that the navy thought she should retire. "I knew that she was not going to be happy to hear this," Sutherland recalled. "She was like Rickover, she was certain the navy couldn't really do without her."[2] She may have been right. Sutherland also commented after Hopper was named commodore, "I remember I thought at the time that this promotion was strictly

Hopper served in the navy under nine different US presidents throughout the course of her military career.

political. . . . But she probably did have more of an influence on computers in the navy than I'm willing to give her."[3]

At her request, Hopper's August 14, 1986, retirement ceremony took place aboard the USS *Constitution*. More than 275 friends, family, and colleagues attended. "I love this ship," Hopper said of the *Constitution*. "She's the beginning of a great tradition. The oldest commissioned ship in the navy. And I'm the oldest officer on active duty. We belong together."[4] During the ceremony, Hopper received the Department of Defense's

Secretary of the Navy John Lehman honored Rear Admiral Hopper at her retirement celebration on August 14, 1986, in Boston, Massachusetts.

Winning the National Medal of Technology

In September 1991, Hopper was awarded the National Medal of Technology. The medal is considered the highest honor of its type in the United States. Hopper was the first woman to receive the award individually, which was for "pioneering accomplishments in the development of computer programming languages [which] simplified computer technology and opened the door to a significantly wider audience of users."[6] Hopper's health kept her from attending the ceremony, where President George H. W. Bush noted that Hopper had "put personal computers on the desks of millions of Americans—and dragged even this president into the computer age."[7] Hopper's written acceptance remarks for the award noted, "If you ask me what accomplishment I'm most proud of, the answer would be all of the young people I've trained over the years; that's more important than writing the first compiler."[8]

highest honor, the Defense Distinguished Service Medal. Hopper repeated one of her key sayings in remarks at the ceremony. "The only phrase I've ever disliked is, 'Why, we've always done it that way.' I always tell young people, 'Go ahead and do it. You can always apologize later.'"[5]

Hopper's retirement from the navy coincided with a new job. In September 1986, she became a senior consultant for Digital Equipment Corporation's (DEC) Government Systems Group. Hopper said of her decision, "You live longer if you stay active and don't retire. When you don't have any contact with people, especially bright, young ones, and are making no more contributions to society, you fall apart."[9] Hopper continued to

The USS *Hopper*, named after Grace Hopper, is an Arleigh Burke–class guided-missile destroyer.

work a heavy travel schedule at DEC. Between 1986 and 1990, she traveled 200 days per year, speaking at colleges, universities, and computer science and engineering gatherings. Her messages continued to evolve just as computers did. She was talking of

handheld computers being able to work as portable checkbooks or portable offices years before such devices existed. Hopper broke her arm in a fall at Washington, DC's Dulles airport in

The Grace Hopper Celebration of Women in Computing

Hopper's work is the inspiration behind the Grace Hopper Celebration of Women in Computing. This three-day annual event is the world's largest gathering of female technologists and is designed to help women in technology learn, exchange ideas, and connect with one another. Technology companies also can attend the conference to recruit new employees. Conference organizers say the conference is especially important for its role in helping women in computer science stay connected, as research shows that a network contributes to women staying in technology fields.

October 1990, and the injury finally forced her to limit her travel.

Hopper's remarkable life came to a close on January 1, 1992. She died in her sleep of natural causes at her home in Arlington, Virginia. She was 85 and still working as a senior consultant with DEC. Family members said she had been in poor health in the days leading up to her death. She was buried with full military honors at Arlington National Cemetery. Her DEC assistant, Rita Yavinsky, recalled a special detail of the funeral. "Grace was such a lady, she got that from her mother," Yavinsky said. "She must have had 5,000 pairs of gloves; in fact, we put a pair of gloves in her casket."[10] In late 1992, the navy announced that it would commission a ship, the USS *Hopper*, in honor of Hopper's 40 years of service to the navy, and the ship went into service in 1995. The USS *Hopper* maintains its home base in Hawaii, where the Pearl Harbor attack spurred its namesake to enter the military. Also like its namesake, it continues to be one of the most advanced of the navy's ships in terms of technology. And in 2017, Yale University announced it would rename its Calhoun College Grace Murray Hopper College.

Hopper received an especially appropriate memorial in December 2013. The Google search engine honored her with a Google doodle on what would have been her 107th birthday. Hopper's Google doodle, which altered the company's famous logo, featured a cartoon of Hopper writing a funny COBOL program. The program referenced Hopper's groundbreaking innovation of turning human communications into something a computer could understand. In this example, the code was SUBTRACT BirthYear FROM CurrentYear Giving Age. Of course the result came back as "107."[11]

Previously, Hopper had said that she wanted to live until the year 2000. "I have two reasons," she said of that wish. "The first is that the party on December 31, 1999, will be a New Year's Eve party to end all New Year's Eve parties. The second is that I want to point back to the early days of computers and say to all the doubters, 'See? We told you the computer could do all that.'"[12]

TIMELINE

1906
Grace Brewster Murray is born in New York, New York, on December 9.

1924
Hopper begins studies at Vassar College in Poughkeepsie, New York.

1928
Hopper graduates with honors from Vassar College with a double major in math and physics; she begins a Vassar College Fellowship at Yale University in New Haven, Connecticut.

1930
Hopper graduates from Yale with a master's degree in mathematics and marries Vincent Hopper in June.

1934
Hopper earns a PhD in mathematics from Yale.

1941
Japanese forces attack the US naval base at Pearl Harbor, Hawaii, in December; Hopper and Vincent agree to separate.

1943
Hopper is sworn into the navy's WAVES program in December.

1944
In July, Hopper joins the Bureau of Ordnance Computation Project at Harvard University in Cambridge, Massachusetts, as a lieutenant, junior grade.

1949

While still in the naval reserves, Hopper joins Eckert-Mauchly Computer Corporation (EMCC) in Philadelphia, Pennsylvania, as a senior mathematician. EMCC is subsequently purchased by Remington Rand.

1955

Sperry Corporation acquires Remington Rand, and Hopper continues her work on software for the UNIVAC machine within the Remington Rand Division.

1967

Hopper again reports for active duty in the navy, where she is a commander.

1969

Hopper is recognized with the Computer Sciences Man of the Year award by the Data Processing Management Association.

1971

Hopper retires from the navy for the second time.

1973

Hopper is promoted to captain.

1983

Hopper is promoted to commodore, which becomes rear admiral, lower half, in 1985.

1986

Hopper retires from the navy for a third time and becomes a senior consultant for Digital Equipment Corporation (DEC).

1992

Hopper dies of natural causes in her home in Arlington, Virginia, on January 1.

ESSENTIAL
FACTS

DATE OF BIRTH
December 9, 1906

PLACE OF BIRTH
New York, New York

DATE OF DEATH
January 1, 1992

PARENTS
Walter Fletcher Murray and Mary Campbell Van Horne Murray

EDUCATION
Graham School
Miss Mary Schoonmaker's School
Hartridge School
Vassar College
Yale University

MARRIAGE
Vincent Hopper (married 1930, divorced 1945)

CAREER HIGHLIGHTS
- Hopper began teaching mathematics at Vassar College in 1931. She enlisted with the US Navy WAVES in 1943 and was assigned to a project at the Harvard Cruft Lab programming the Mark I. She helped program the Mark II, and began creating subroutines that would speed up the coding process of computers.

- In 1949, Hopper began writing coding instructions for the BINAC, the world's first computer to use stored programs. She became head of the software division at Eckert-Mauchly Computer Corporation and programmed the

UNIVAC. By 1952, Hopper and her team had created the A-0, a compiler which led to the popular COBOL computer-programming language.

- Hopper retired from the navy for the final time in 1986.

SOCIETAL CONTRIBUTIONS

- Hopper developed computer-programming innovations that dramatically improved the accessibility of computers to more programmers, and ultimately, more consumers.
- Hopper spearheaded the early migration of computers from science and military applications to business use.
- Throughout her career, Hopper continued to teach and was a lifelong advocate of computer science as a career choice for young people.

CONFLICTS

- Hopper is recognized as a pioneer in a male-dominated profession, becoming one of the first female computer programmers.
- In 1923, Hopper failed the Latin exam portion of the entrance exams to Vassar College. She returned to school and retook the exam one year later, passing and gaining entrance into Vassar.
- Hopper failed her US Navy WAVES physical exam because she was 16 pounds underweight for her height, according to navy guidelines. She had to argue her case and secure a waiver before being accepted.
- Mid-career, she struggled with alcohol abuse and depression until friends stepped in to assist her with getting professional help.

QUOTE

"The only phrase I've ever disliked is, 'Why, we've always done it that way.' I always tell young people, 'Go ahead and do it. You can always apologize later.'"—*Grace Hopper*

GLOSSARY

algebra
A type of mathematics in which symbols and letters are used to represent unknown numbers.

alma mater
The school, college, or university that a person attended.

application
A computer program that performs a certain task.

ballistics
The science of projectiles and firearms.

binary
A numerical system that has two as a base instead of ten.

COBOL
A computer-programming language designed for business use, it stands for common business-oriented language.

compiler
A computer program or set of programs that changes source code written in a programming language into another computer language, usually binary.

cosine
The ratio of the side that is nearest an acute angle in a right triangle to the long side (called the hypotenuse).

diode
A semiconductor device that allows the flow of electric current in one direction.

displacement
To take the place of something else.

encrypt
To convert information into a cipher or code to prevent unauthorized access.

enlisted
Enrolled in the armed services.

geometry
The branch of mathematics that deals with lines, angles, shapes, etc.

in absentia
Without being present.

input
Information fed into a computer.

mainframe
A large and very powerful computer.

microcomputer
A computer that sits on a desk or can be carried in a case.

output
Information produced by a computer.

relay
An electrical device that is activated by a current or signal in one circuit to open or close another circuit.

trigonometry
The branch of mathematics dealing with the relationships between the sides and angles of triangles.

ADDITIONAL
RESOURCES

SELECTED BIBLIOGRAPHY

Beyer, Kurt. *Grace Hopper and the Invention of the Information Age.* Cambridge, MA: MIT, 2009. Print.

Isaacson, Walter. *The Innovators: How a Group of Hackers, Geniuses, and Geeks Created the Digital Revolution.* New York: Simon, 2014. Print.

Mitchell, Carmen L. "The Contributions of Grace Murray Hopper to Computer Science and Computer Education." Diss. U of North Texas, 1994. *University of North Texas Library.* Web. 25 Jan. 2017.

Williams, Kathleen Broome. *Grace Hopper: Admiral of the Cyber Sea.* Annapolis, MD: Naval Institute, 2004. Print.

FURTHER READINGS

Anderson, Kane. *Power of Patterns: Coding.* Huntington Beach, CA: Teacher Create Materials, 2017. Print.

Swaby, Rachel. *Trailblazers: 33 Women in Science Who Changed the World.* New York: Delacorte, 2016. Print.

WEBSITES

To learn more about Women in Science, visit **abdobooklinks.com**. These links are routinely monitored and updated to provide the most current information available.

FOR MORE INFORMATION

For more information on this subject, contact or visit the following organizations:

Grace Hopper Museum
Grace Murray Hopper Service Center
1482 Read Road
San Diego, California
619-545-8550
http://www.public.navy.mil/fcc-c10f/nctssandiego/Pages/Museums.aspx
The Grace Hopper Museum celebrates the evolution of naval communications and is located in the Grace Murray Hopper Service Center in San Diego, California. A collection of photos and displays of older communications equipment includes a glimpse into the history of data processing in the navy.

Harvard University Science Center
1 Oxford Street, B11
Cambridge, MA 02138
617-495-2653
http://scictr.fas.harvard.edu
Visitors to Harvard University, where Hopper worked during World War II, can stop by the Science Center and see sections of the original Mark I in the building's lobby. The building also houses the History of Science, Mathematics, and Statistics Departments.

SOURCE
NOTES

CHAPTER 1. THERE'S GOT TO BE A BETTER WAY

1. Carmen L. Mitchell. "The Contributions of Grace Murray Hopper to Computer Science and Computer Education." Diss. U of North Texas, 1994. 40. *University of North Texas Library*. Web. 25 Jan. 2017.

2. Ibid. 43.

3. *Fundamentals of Computers*. New Delhi, Ind.: Pearson Education, 2011. 9. *Google Book Search*. Web. 10 Feb. 2017.

4. Kathleen Broome Williams. *Grace Hopper: Admiral of the Cyber Sea*. Annapolis, MD: Naval Institute, 2004. Print. 83.

CHAPTER 2. WELCOME, GRACE

1. Kathleen Broome Williams. *Grace Hopper: Admiral of the Cyber Sea*. Annapolis, MD: Naval Institute, 2004. Print. 2–3.

2. Carmen L. Mitchell. "The Contributions of Grace Murray Hopper to Computer Science and Computer Education." Diss. U of North Texas, 1994. 13. *University of North Texas Library*. Web. 25 Jan. 2017.

3. Kathleen Broome Williams. *Grace Hopper: Admiral of the Cyber Sea*. Annapolis, MD: Naval Institute, 2004. Print. 1, 3.

CHAPTER 3. COLLEGE STUDENT

1. Carmen L. Mitchell. "The Contributions of Grace Murray Hopper to Computer Science and Computer Education." Diss. U of North Texas, 1994. 19. *University of North Texas Library*. Web. 25 Jan. 2017.

2. Ibid. 18–19.

3. "Grace Murray Hopper and Devils, Too." *Vassar Quarterly* 93.1 (1 Dec. 1996). *Vassar College Libraries*. Web. 10 Feb. 2017.

4. Kathleen Broome Williams. *Grace Hopper: Admiral of the Cyber Sea*. Annapolis, MD: Naval Institute, 2004. Print. 11.

CHAPTER 4. BACK TO VASSAR

1. Carmen L. Mitchell. "The Contributions of Grace Murray Hopper to Computer Science and Computer Education." Diss. U of North Texas, 1994. 20. *University of North Texas Library.* Web. 25 Jan. 2017.

2. Kathleen Broome Williams. *Grace Hopper: Admiral of the Cyber Sea.* Annapolis, MD: Naval Institute, 2004. Print. 14.

3. Ibid. 17.

CHAPTER 5. IN THE NAVY

1. Kathleen Broome Williams. *Grace Hopper: Admiral of the Cyber Sea.* Annapolis, MD: Naval Institute Press, 2004. Print. 23.

2. Ibid.

3. Ibid.

4. Ibid. 22.

5. Carmen L. Mitchell. "The Contributions of Grace Murray Hopper to Computer Science and Computer Education." Diss. U of North Texas, 1994. 27. *University of North Texas Library.* Web. 25 Jan. 2017.

6. Ibid.

7. Ibid.

8. Ibid. 28.

CHAPTER 6. AGAINST THE CLOCK, AROUND THE CLOCK

1. Anne B. Keating and Joseph R. Hargitai. *The Wired Professor: A Guide to Incorporating the World Wide Web in College Instruction.* New York: New York UP, 1999. 34. *Google Book Search.* Web. 10 Feb. 2017.

2. Walter Isaacson. *The Innovators: How a Group of Hackers, Geniuses, and Geeks Created the Digital Revolution.* New York: Simon, 2014. Print. 90.

3. Carmen L. Mitchell. "The Contributions of Grace Murray Hopper to Computer Science and Computer Education." Diss. U of North Texas, 1994. 33. *University of North Texas Library.* Web. 25 Jan. 2017.

4. Ibid.

5. Ibid.

6. Kathleen Broome Williams. *Grace Hopper: Admiral of the Cyber Sea.* Annapolis, MD: Naval Institute, 2004. Print. 68–69.

CHAPTER 7. ENTER COBOL

1. Carmen L. Mitchell. "The Contributions of Grace Murray Hopper to Computer Science and Computer Education." Diss. U of North Texas, 1994. 49. *University of North Texas Librar,:* Web. 25 Jan. 2017.

2. Kathleen Broome Williams. *Grace Hopper: Admiral of the Cyber Sea.* Annapolis, MD: Naval Institute, 2004. Print. 86.

3. Ibid. 86–88.

4. Carmen L. Mitchell. "The Contributions of Grace Murray Hopper to Computer Science and Computer Education." Diss. U of North Texas, 1994. 54. *University of North Texas Library.* Web. 25 Jan. 2017.

5. John C. Dvorak. "Whatever Happened to the Seven Dwarfs?—Dwarf Two: Sperry-Rand." *Dvorak Uncensored.* Dvorak News, n.d. Web. 22 Oct. 2016.

6. Kathleen Broome Williams. *Grace Hopper: Admiral of the Cyber Sea.* Annapolis, MD: Naval Institute, 2004. Print. 97.

7. Ibid. 98.

8. Ibid. 180.

9. Ibid.

CHAPTER 8. AT THE PENTAGON

1. Randy Alfred. "Aug. 7, 1944: Still a Few Bugs in the System." *Wired.* Wired, 7 Aug. 2008. Web. 10 Feb. 2017.

2. "What Were the Military and Political Goals Underlying the War in Vietnam?" *Gilder Lehrman Institute of American History.* Gilder Lehrman Institute of American History, 2017. Web. 15 Feb. 2017.

3. Carmen L. Mitchell. "The Contributions of Grace Murray Hopper to Computer Science and Computer Education." Diss. U of North Texas, 1994. 59. *University of North Texas Library.* Web. 25 Jan. 2017.

4. Kurt Beyer. *Grace Hopper and the Invention of the Information Age.* Cambridge, MA: MIT, 2009. Print. 314.

5. Carmen L. Mitchell. "The Contributions of Grace Murray Hopper to Computer Science and Computer Education." Diss. U of North Texas, 1994. 60. *University of North Texas Library.* Web. 25 Jan. 2017.

6. Kathleen Broome Williams. *Grace Hopper: Admiral of the Cyber Sea.* Annapolis, MD: Naval Institute, 2004. Print. 143.

CHAPTER 9. REAR ADMIRAL HOPPER

1. Carmen L. Mitchell. "The Contributions of Grace Murray Hopper to Computer Science and Computer Education." Diss. U of North Texas, 1994. 64. *University of North Texas Library*. Web. 25 Jan. 2017.

2. Ibid. 70.

3. Ibid. 64.

4. Ibid. 70.

5. Ibid. 71.

6. Ibid. 77.

7. George Bush. "Remarks at the Presentation Ceremony for the National Medals of Science and Technology." *American Presidency Project*. American Presidency Project, 16 Sept. 1991. Web. 9 Feb. 2017.

8. Carmen L. Mitchell. "The Contributions of Grace Murray Hopper to Computer Science and Computer Education." Diss. U of North Texas, 1994. 77. *University of North Texas Library*. Web. 25 Jan. 2017.

9. Ibid. 71.

10. Ibid. 78.

11. "Grace Hopper Google Doodle." *Google*. Google, 9 Dec. 2013. Web. 9 Feb. 2017.

12. John Markoff. "Rear Adm. Grace M. Hopper Dies; Innovator in Computers was 85." *New York Times*. New York Times, 2 Jan. 1992. Web. 25 Jan. 2017.

INDEX

ABOUT THE
AUTHOR

Jill Wheeler is the author of nearly 300 nonfiction books for young readers, covering everything from science and environmental topics to biographies of celebrities. In addition to her writing, she stays busy working in sustainability for an agricultural company. Wheeler lives in Minneapolis, Minnesota, with her husband and whichever of their three adult daughters happens to be visiting at the time.